Evernote For Beginners:

Evernote Essential Tips to Accomplish Your Goals, Remember Everything, Organize and Simplify Your Life

By

Dale Blake

Table of Contents

Evernote For Beginners: Evernote Essential Tips to
Accomplish Your Goals, Remember Everything,
Organize and Simplify Your Life

By Dale Blake

© Copyright 2014 Dale Blake

First Published, 2014

Printed in the United States of America

Introduction

Change has led people of this time to become diverse in many different aspects – in terms of goals, beliefs, and practices, all manifested in a wide array of different lifestyles. Unlike before, parents now work online from home; students seek for video-call-assisted teaching tasks; call center agents increase in number; health care professionals utilize mobile apps to improve in their field; even children have become technically adept. Regardless of the differences people of this generation have in so many aspects, what seems to be common today are the necessity of the use of the products of technology, and the universal goal of saving time, money, energy, and even the earth itself have turned into concrete advocacies.

While some blame technology for these needs, it is the same that seeks to address them in order for human beings to achieve such goal. For instance, various inventions and innovations have been embarked on by scientists and laymen alike. Some come up with recycled gadgets, some with more efficient systems to operate, and others, with simple life hacks. Many also create or support certain applications that subscribe to saving such essential resources, which are accessible to what has been mostly occupying your hands: the mobile phone.

Evernote, a 'virtual notebook' as some would call it, is one of technology's breakthroughs in involving itself in your way to respond to such needs – perhaps unknowingly. It may be install in a computer, in a mobile gadget, or in both. Other than its characteristics of being accessible and environment-friendly, this app is also amazingly useful and user-friendly. It labels itself as "the modern workspace that helps you be your most productive self." No wonder, it has gained the title, New York Times 'Top 10 Must-Have App', and has emerged winner in the TechCrunch Crunchies, the Mashable Awards and the Webbys.

Chapter 1. How to Get Started

To some, using Evernote may seem overwhelming at first, perhaps because of its breath-taking features, but just like any other useful app, it is rather simple and easy to maximize its beneficial functions, even for beginners. Included in what follows are key procedures on starting with your experience of one of the most productive apps ever created in your computer, and ways to maximize nearly everything it offers for an organized living towards the attainment of your life's goals.

1. Installing the software

Using Evernote in your computer allows you to maximize its magic in the most complete way. Installing it in your PC, takes only around a couple of minutes or so, may it be a Windows PC or a Macintosh. You only have to visit the Evernote website which will provide you with the correct download option, as it will instantly determine the kind of computer you are using. If you are a Windows user, you may download the setup executable file where you choose to place it, then you may launch the setup program when the download completes. If you are a Mac user download and install Evernote as it is, by following the simple instructions provided.

2. Setting up your personal account

After having launched the app on your PC for the first time, you may create a new Evernote account by clicking "Get a free Evernote account now". Upon doing so, just like signing up for a new email account, only much simpler, fill out all the fields requiring your information, as well as a unique username and a password, to create the account and to log you in Evernote. It is important that you remember your username and password, while keeping the former unique, and making sure the latter is neither obvious nor easy to guess in order to ensure privacy and security. Remember that if you are to use the app as a personal journal, a planner, an album, or a combination of these and more, what you store in it reveals much of your identity, that of your work, and that of your social circle. So unless you do not mind having your precious data exposed, take extra measures to secure them, as you would your inbox.

3. Creating your first 'note'

One of the most amazing things about Evernote is that you may store in it many different kinds of content in it, such as photos of receipts, of travels, of wish lists, and of more, as well as simple text, the most common of them. Simple texts may be an expression of your ideas, which you refuse to make momentary, an email you would like to keep, more than label as favourite, or part of a webpage you would want to remember, rather than merely save as bookmark.

In order to create an Evernote document, which you may call your 'note', click on the button labelled "New Note" at the top of the main window. This will lead you to a page with a field for a note title and a body, with options for the font type, size and color. The tool bar also includes options to bold, italicize or underline the text, and to adjust paragraph alignment. With all these provisions, you may now input the title of your first note, and write down your thoughts on the body of the note. In case you have data copied to your clipboard, on the other hand, you may paste them on the same body.

In case you would want to save web content as a note, Evernote has made it remarkably possible, as you may also do so with the use of the Evernote Web Clipper. All you have to do is to highlight the web content you wish to save, and click on the Evernote button in your browser toolbar. (In the case of the use of Internet Explorer, just right click on the highlighted content you wish to save, and confirm the command.) By doing so, Evernote creates a new note containing the part of the website you highlighted. You may edit according to your preference.

The details of your new note are saved automatically by the application.

4. Adding things you see and/or hear

One of Evernote's taglines is "capture anything." It elaborates that you may save your ideas, things you like, things you hear, and things you see. The many types of content Evernote can store, as mentioned earlier, include all kinds of images that you may want to keep for even longer than a lifetime. In order to add photos of your most memorable moments, of that wardrobe you are saving up for, of receipts to monitor your expenses, or of business cards you collected from prospective business partners, all you have to do is to click that "New Note" button as you did in creating your first document, locate the image file in your PC storage, then drag the image directly into the note body. If you are saving photos from the web, you may proceed with the same click-drag procedure. As it claims to capture and store 'anything', including what you see and/or hear, Evernote may also keep audio and video files just the same.

5. Creating a to-do list

Apart from its amazing note-taking and cloud-storage features, Evernote also brags of its neat capacity to set a prompt for any note, which is equally easy to do. You only need to open the note, tap the Reminder icon, and set a due date for time-sensitive reminders. All these notes categorized as reminders will show up in a To-do List above your Note List, where you may practice your organizing skills by editing or sorting them according to themes or chronology, depending on your needs. You may also check off a completed task in the Reminders List by clicking on the checkbox, as you probably do in paper, without deleting the original note.

6. Going mobile

Accessibility and portability matter. While the app has the most complete version in desktop, it does not neglect the almost obligatory to-go characteristic of the people of this time. What makes Evernote even more awesome is that you may also install it on your smart phone. You may access the same account but logging in with your username and password, and enjoy its great features literally anywhere. There is no rule however, that states that installing the app in your computer is a prerequisite to accessing it on your mobile. In fact, you may create your account on any smart phone, and access your notes in any other computer just the same. What matters is that you have your account, and that you access it through any device that is internet-ready and Evernote-capable – nearly any gadget, that is.

7. Discovering the magic of syncing

The second part of the tagline, "capture everything", which allows you to store your notes bearing various content, is "access anywhere". Evernote claims it has the ability "to work on nearly every computer, phone and mobile device out there". This works by an automatic synchronization feature of the app, which may be annually controlled by clicking the "Sync" button. The mechanism by which this is possible basically lies on its being a 'cloud-stored notebook'.

The term cloud, as used by the more techie persons, may be easiest understood by seeing it as that which represents the indefinable yet universal nature of the worldwide web. As such, Evernote synchronization takes place as all the notes you create in your account are stored through the internet in this cloud, which is accessible through any Evernote-capable and internet-capable device to which you log in your account.

Having your notes synchronized is beneficial in many circumstances such as when you may update in the to-do list you have encoded using your personal computer at home, the tasks you have accomplished at the office by accessing the note on your smart phone, rather than having to carry the bulky desktop at work. You may also check on the photo of the wardrobe you want from a website to compare it with what you saw in a mall, even if you saved that image from home. You can even save an audio file of a meeting using your Evernote-capable multimedia device and transcribe the minutes of the meeting at a coffee shop where you can focus more, using your laptop.

In other words, Evernote has designed itself to be portable, allowing you to access your account, hence all your notes by using any device in which you log in to the same account.

Chapter 2. How to Get More Out of It

While there are Evernote-compatible products and services that may be checked out at the Evernote Trunk, and further assistance on maximizing the app that is available by accessing its official Knowledge Base for a support team to address your concerns, there are even more basic ways to get the most out of Evernote before you would opt to resort to these useful attributes.

1. A customized and flexible workplace

For one, taking notes has become very handy as the app allows you to write in workplaces you can design for yourself depending on your current needs or moods. The incredible portability of use of this so-called virtual notebook, which in fact could be an understatement of its wonder, enables you to bring your essential stuff anywhere you want. In fact, using the app is not even limited to work-related matters; it extends to keeping a personal planner, a receipt storage, an intimate journal, or even an album of past, present and future memories – anything you want for a storage. Nonetheless, it not only works as such storage, but as a means to get things done, while securing important data be it receipts, bills and invoices, reservations and tickets for business or personal travel, secret recipes you need to remember, or intimate reflections only you should access.

2. A convenient way to get organized

Along with the neat To-do List the app has going, one of the main features of Evernote is allowing you to maintain categories by compiling notes into different notebooks and by using tags to be more systematic. This allows your so-called 'virtual notebook' to become a virtual personal library. By having this, a very convenient cataloguing system is provided by its highlight of finding anything quickly, as texts, photos and PDFs, among others, are searchable. This means that you only have to enter a keyword from the note you are looking for and the app will lead you to entries containing the same.

While most would probably go for the above approach, which has become the popular one, some take other strategies of being relatively 'organized', taking advantage of the finding-anything-fast feature the app offers. One approach for this, if you are not the obsessive-compulsive type, is to maintain two notebooks – one for your temporary files (those that still need some finishing touch) and another for your permanent files (those that do not need further editing). Of course this means that all your permanent notes are in one notebook altogether, but users of this technique argue that that anything can be found by clicking the search button makes it still manageable.

To combine both styles, you may also consider maintaining one notebook for temporary notes and a notebook for each category of all your permanent files. Both the wisdom from the conventional way, and the trick of keeping a notebook for half-baked files, are there. Whichever approach you choose would work though, for as long as it suits you best.

3. An opportunity to share

Evernote seems to believe that the good stuff is meant to be shared; in fact, it makes its presence felt in society by being part of your daily social life. It not only facilitates note-taking, file storage and planning, but also encourages you to share your ideas and resources to others – may they be family members, friends, colleagues, clients or constituents – who also have an

Evernote account. This is made possible with the use of the shared notebooks feature, which you can control manually.

In the workplace, doing so creates an opportunity to collaborate in doing tasks and to simplify transactions, while saving essential resources such as time, energy and money. In the more personal social realm, moreover, sharing day-to-day ideas, experiences, feelings, and even just little things, could maintain, if not deepen relationships with people who matter.

4. An earth-saving advocacy to be part of

Using Evernote makes you part of the community that subscribes to paperless productivity. Supporting the 'paperless advocacy' allows you to contribute to the reduction of the following, among others: a) business and personal costs, b) use of filing cabinets, c) office space, d) waiting time for clients, e) inefficiency brought about by searching for hard files, and f) risks in losing valuable data. The most remarkable of all the advantages of going paperless, however, is the opportunity to protect the environment.

What the use of Evernote, and using paper plates, recycling plastic bottles and segregating waste materials have in common is saving the earth. How the app contributes to the seemingly enormous goal is its support for paperless productivity by turning paper documents into electric ones. Paperless productivity is said to be a simple way to have a huge impact in helping rescue your habitat. By reducing the need to use paper, hence the need for its production, you get to help reduce carbon dioxide emission, decreasing further damage to Mother Nature.

While a simple cloud note-taking activity using the app may seem to you as a tiny means towards such a big end, think about how many people can be involved in this worthwhile advocacy without some of them even knowing. The mere act of storing documents in the cloud, rather than printing them out and reproducing hard copies to file, may indeed appear small, but if you could look into how this simple move can impact a healthier world for the next generations through a paperless future, you will be able to appreciate the realization that the use a simple and affordable app (it's free at 60 MB) makes you morally responsible.

Chapter 3. Additional Tips

Other than the manifest benefits of using Evernote at work already mentioned, it has other significantly infinite advantages anyone of any disposition can relate with. Most important of which is its paramount importance to the user to innovate, to infuse, to ingather and to influence.

1. Innovate

The accessibility of Evernote is valuable in expressing creativity— be it thoughts (ideas), photos taken or just about anything you wish to express. If you wish to keep details of an idea (a poem, an article, a song or an anecdote), make a note of a memory in the past or of the present experiences, chronicle your everyday encounters (journals or diaries), or document through photos your priceless moments, Evernote is the perfect avenue to make all these possible within your reach. Evernote's convenience can bring you to just anywhere as far as your imagination brings. It captures both momentous or trivial 'anything' you select that it receives. Creativity is harnessed using Evernote through simple expressions of concepts you have in mind. Moreover, as you habitually do it, skills are further developed capitalizing on the organizational skills you eventually imbibe as implicit in the regular use of it. As you determine what Evernote records, you dictate its substance. Indeed, man is the measure of all things. It is this capability of the human person to transcend borders in expressing ideas that Evernote also seizes as it captures all things of which are, how they are and which are not, how they are not, all are commensurate to the user's being the measure of all things.

2. Infuse

As thoughts are readily articulated using Evernote, the use of this app also gives you a readily available access to permeate the files saved when you wish to add, revise, change or discard them. Sometimes, important ideas come during the wee hours in the morning, the time you least expect them. But because connecting to Evernote is effortless and undemanding, doing so is also trouble-free. Want to take a photo of a nice view you rarely see? Capture it and save it in Evernote, you capture each memory including the exact details of the captured moment, by including a caption such as the date, place of occurrence, mood, people involved or any other facts or details which may be relevant to include in the caption of the photo/s taken – easy and free. While gaining access to it may be easy which normally jeopardizes protection to users, Evernote still ensures security of access premising on the fact that you create your own account, deciding on the details of it such as email address, username and above all a required password. Therefore, all Evernote users are entitled the basic protection especially for files or notes that need confidentiality.

3. Ingather (Converge)

Evernote can be a compilation of a hodgepodge of just about anything about you and your ideas including your plans for the day, week, month or the whole year. Evernote can serve as your virtual planner (for Evernote on smartphones) that helps you to be more organized and prepared for the things that you should do; in particular, you can key in the grocery items or any other essentials you plan to buy for everyday necessities or things to buy for special occasions such as Birthdays, Christmas Day, Thanksgiving Day, among others. It is also best to use Evernote in keeping reminders of important dates like the schedule of payments for monthly bills, birthdates of important people, deadlines for tasks or just a simple reminder to yourself to 'seize the day' (Carpe Diem). Anything can be converged in this state of the art application with as much as one hundred thousand (100,000) notes for Free category, another one hundred thousand notes for Premium category, five hundred thousand notes per company account for Evernote Business category to be compiled. Evernote is basically a divergence of a limitless ideas put together encapsulating you and your thoughts.

It is unquestionable that its ingeniousness and practicality make up its most important features that people today whose reliance to technology equates to user-friendliness and efficiency that people of all ages can easily comprehend.

4. Influence

Convergence, as one important benefit of using Evernote, connects to its other benefit which is to influence. While you keep a personal copy of the personal files saved in your Evernote account, sharing of notes is also available. This is an option which may be beneficial to students, professionals or practically anyone who wish to share files to others. Through this, working together may be less complicated. For a student who uses technology in researching, making projects, jotting down notes, and others, saving files for these purposes may be done through Evernote. Sharing the same may also be done when one wishes to. Sharing individual notes to friends or other people is on hand through Evernote. Moreover, companies who maintain Evernote Business accounts may take advantage of this special feature of Evernote to share files with people or companies they work with through the simple steps of sharing using work chat. Acknowledging that no man is an island, in return, other users can also share their files which may be useful to you. Ideas may be derived from others users' files that you can get ideas from developing a mutual purpose of propagating ideas to the Evernote community. There is reciprocal relationship built among Evernote users, the power of sharing, indeed.

With this selection given to the user, it is implicit in the sharing capability the underlying potential to influence other people especially those to whom the notes or files shared spread through. It can be both positive and negative (like any other technology) that a user can influence other people. That is why it is important that users share by giving out files responsibly. Responsibility begets responsibility.

While doing the aforementioned options of sharing may be a peril to a responsible use of technology and internet access, Evernote provides options for its users in managing their sharing capabilities. This implies that Evernote shares the accountability with its users to the responsible use of their identity represented by the notes or files they share to the public. It goes without saying that Evernote also promotes consideration of the users' moral responsibility in handling their accounts.

Final Words

Using Evernote to simply take notes and access them anywhere, plan systematically, share ideas and resources, employ creativity, manage expenses, and keep memories, will indeed bring out the productive, organized and earth-loving human in you. Doing so will not only help you accomplish your personal and professional goals in life, but will also influence you in organizing your day-to-day living.

With the fast-changing time, every single second must be worthy of your effort. Time is gold as they say. Therefore, to waste your precious time may be a waste of time. Having said this, it is crucial to consider what options to be taken in order to make the most out of your time by organizing your everyday to achieve your goals. The use of Evernote, with its unique and special features being your virtual memory bank, helps you in fulfilling these vital minutiae of every single moment because every second counts.

Thank You Page

I want to personally thank you for reading my book. I hope you found information in this book useful and I would be very grateful if you could leave your honest review about this book. I certainly want to thank you in advance for doing this.